Particular Sunlights

PARTICULAR SUNLIGHTS

John Loveday

John Loveday

— for Sue

HEADLAND

Some to the memory of my mother and father,
some for Evelyn

ISBN 0 903074 47 8

First published in 1986 by
HEADLAND PUBLICATIONS
38 York Avenue
West Kirby
Wirral
Merseyside L48 3JF

Set in Garamond Book by
Angus Graham Associates
Reading, Berkshire

Contents

Acknowledgements

Some of these poems were first published in *Encounter, London Magazine, New Poetry* (Arts Council/PEN), *Over the Bridge* (Penguin Books), *Poems for Poetry 84* (The Poetry Society), *Poesie Europe, Poetry Review, Winter Dragoncards* (Mandeville Press), *Workshop New Poetry.* Some were broadcast by the B.B.C. in *Poetry Now* (Radio 3), *Time for Verse* (Radio 4) or *Friday Looking Sideways* (Television, South). 'Under the Yew Tree' was illustrated as a poem poster by Paul Peter Piech. 'The Bowl of Milk' was commissioned by the Tate Gallery and published in *With a Poet's Eye* (Tate Gallery, 1986). Seven of the poems were collected in *Particularities* (Priapus Press, 1977), four are from *Bones and Angels* (Mid-Day Publications, 1978), three from *The Agricultural Engineer* (Priapus Press, 1982), and thirteen comprised *From the Old Foundry* (Mandeville Press, 1983). Grateful acknowledgements for these pamphlet publications are made to John Cotton, Anne Stevenson, Peter Scupham and John Mole.

Particularities

On a Drawing by Czar Alexander II of his Mistress, Catherine

A classic pose: and yet
A breast too well defined,
The pubic cleft drawn high,
Too prominent, in dark
Emphatic hair, proclaim,
So far from classic calm,
The turbulent amateur.

The thin wife coughed downstairs.
Feet of children fretted
Vast floors. Their voices called
In corridors, remote
Or near and still far off
From her. We are not yours,
Not yours. She coughed, dribbled
A ruby in the bowl.

These lines were flesh. She dreamed,
Perhaps, some garret girl's.
The sweet usurper lay,
Silks slipped, and history.
Russia was elsewhere. They
Are closer to us here
Than Tolstoy in his shirt
Could ever be.

Under the Yew Tree

The man who threshed the corn,
The man who milled it,
Lie close here.
The yew tree shadows both,
Is old:
Its roots will not disturb
The man who threshed the corn,
My father, Tom,
Or Billy with one arm,
The man who milled it.

Arcady

Bright poppies in brown corn;
A silent pond, the red-finned roach
Cold in your hand; orchards,
Long grass; old cottages
Crumbling among staked scarlet runners,
Peas, black oozing plums:

A small girl naked by
A summer road, the Arcady
You travelled from still close
About her toes, her hair,
The red wound like a burn
Your memory has never healed.

Reeds

These reeds, in this wind:
Particularities
Define our lives.

In fancy, too:
The girl, a red scarf on her head,
Crosses the bridge.
A touch establishes,
Others would alter her.
A different girl, a bridge
To somewhere else.

Not Once

Not once in thirty years had I remembered you.
You were nothing at all to me,
Quite unmemorable:
Not for one day a childhood sweetheart even,
A plain girl only, with yellow hair
Cropped straight, the voice of a boy.

Yet this morning a dream brought you,
Unaccountably,
Ten years older, perhaps beautiful:
An image I did not know, and cold sense says
Was never true.

Nendell's Inn

Portland, Oregon. The new motel.
We breakfast by a window, looking down
On water, ducks, grey willows.
They surprise. Sharp leaves flicker
A Norfolk sunlight, forty years
Beyond these vast horizons. Lives,
Remoter now than distance, time,
Alone can make them, move out there,
Voices under the water,
A face in the trees.

A Suggested Theme

'...leaving, in time,
the house of Passion'.

A shy girl's face at a high window:
'Are you going, my love? Going?'

By the darkened doorway, another woman:
'Go! Go!'

from *Bones & Angels*
& *The Agricultural Engineer*

Skeleton

Ubiquitous as bone, the word,
At six or eight, is 'skellington'.
They hear it so, learn later to
Discriminate. They also write
Of flying 'brids', and 'littel grils':
Transpose, almost to rule.
                                    Along
The nerves the messages run true,
In time. The birds come down to earth.
The girls have grown. Somewhere, still waits,
However spelt, the skellington.

Imaginary Company

for my daughter Sharon

'...transitional phenomena'
D.W. Winnicott, *Play and Reality*

The Kim, the Conch, the Ditchman, Agony,
The Baby, and the Piece of Glass: these were
The imaginary company you kept
When you first talked. The Kim we understood.
He (it?) came first, was small enough
To close your hand on, did as he was told,
Seemed genial, a gentle friend. We shared
His presence with you, let him sit on chairs —
A blind impending bum warned sharply off —
And always listened to his small affairs.

The conch came shortly after. 'Kim'n-Conch':
You spoke their names as composite; they seemed
At times one character. What most intrigued
Was that we knew you'd never heard the word.
Then came the Ditchman. We lived where
Few ditches were. He came from no real place,
Appeared a name only, a small Godot,
Or figure from some quaint Morality.
Our fancy fleshed him, but he never lost
Strangeness. The next to come was Agony.

The word's odd metamorphosis amazed.
It lilted on your tongue. 'Where's Agony?'
I made my Greco joke, that *Agony*
Was *in the Garden*. You knew otherwise.
You saw them all as clear as you saw us,
For that brief while, my dear transitional
Worldling. Today, no hint of memory
Remains. You nurse your own firstborn. We see
Him climb to glimmering consciousness.
Behind him climbs — what dark mythology?

Mowing

Grass almost mown. 'Neighbours
Have lawns,' my child said; 'we
Have grass.' Some time ago.
And some time, too, since this
Sharp other memory
I make in circling
The dwindling patch of weed,
Our 'grass':
    cornfield, the sun
Well down, the brown-armed men,
The binder homing in,
The cudgel in my hand,
The moment when, blindly,
The rabbits run.
     Gladly,
I never caught one, would
Have panicked at the small
Maimed struggler, not held
It right, bungled the blow
To kill.
    They were so sure.
So competent, in their
Restricted compass; grown
Too far away now, I
Can but reach them dumbly on
These random pages, lean
Thirty-odd-shilling men.

Grass almost mown. Nothing
Will run but words, blindly.
Let them run well.

Shaping It

Words are the hardest things
    for shaping it.

Paint would be so much easier,
    with light and dark,
    a tint of rose;

Or stone,
    carved to an egg's smoothness;

Wood, perhaps,
    a found shape, wanting only
    the chisel's emphasis,
    grained and grooved,
    evocative;

Clay,
    the fingers' element;

Undulant lines of a delicate pencil.

Flesh would be best,
    plump on fine bone,

        though transient.

from *The Agricultural Engineer*

March

A willow is down in the pond, the steam engine winding
Taut wire rope, to drag it away.
Slowly it follows, minute red roots in the water showing,
Already, at every node, that it wants to stay.

May

The quick blade's scream
Across the orchard; gleam
Of naked poplar, elm;
Soft sawdust piled at dusk.

July

Old threshing drums new-painted,
Yellow as this year's corn;
Red and green offsetting —
Poppy and thorn.

From the Old Foundry

The Old Foundry

Strange, how, after an evening of wanting to write,
And no thought coming that seemed worth a word,
There should lie, suddenly, in a November night,
That dusty road and the long facade
Of the old foundry, through clear sunlight
Of a day from childhood. Strange, and right.

The Path

I take the backdoor way, the house I coveted,
And won by work, a bit too grand.
I go like a tradesman, by the side —
And am a tradesman, too, I work
At eighty-six still when there's work to do.
There's not much, though, if truth be told:
Each day I go to *be* there,
Shuffle like this through the grass,
This path I made by walking it.
Not too much longer now: I hear
Them bells on Sundays, hate that sound,
Told John, my grandson, I don't want
To go, don't want to leave the world,
Lie over there, where Edith . . .
She was beautiful; ten children, though,
And time . . . and still her legs,
Old woman's legs, unveined . . .
Oh God, corruption now! Walk faster,
Put that thought behind, behind.
Path-end and now the road, my stick
Tap, tap, I step it out, here comes
Old Cuckoo, stick and bowler hat,
That nickname all my life, *cocoa*
I should have read but said *cuckoo,*
And how they laughed . . .

And most are dead, they don't laugh now,
While I still work — my good machines,
My foundry, ledgers, bills — strong yet,
Old Cuckoo on his way to work,
A sort of permanence if they
Remember, stick and bowler hat,
My path still there when I am not.

The Water-Butt

A narrow space: enough for an elder tree
To grow, between two walls, a third behind.
A scatter of rusting things, the small debris
Of workshop, foundry; nettles; and, in front,
A cylinder of iron: boiler torn
From some old traction engine, left to be
A makeshift water-butt. It filled with rain
From iron roof-troughs, gave an orange fringe
Of new rust to the water's scaly green.

Red squiggling larvae gleamed. Tap at the rim,
Minute heads turned, and down they scuttled at
The first vibration, gone as one, to swim
Back almost instantly, and hang there. Tap,
And down they went again, up as before
A moment afterwards. They did not learn.
The child also: their name; why they would go
Yet rise so quickly; how they came there, went;
What they — or he — would change into.

The Privy

He sat foursquare, elbows
Upon his thighs, and eased
Himself, a whitewashed wall
Behind, on either side,
In front the whitewashed door.

A fly buzzed patiently,
Waiting to drop again,
Resume. Below the hole,
An ancient mound, a space,
The dangling genital
He never used, loner
And misfit, cripple, tramp,
The simple, runaway —
A composite of odd
Itinerants. They all
Sat here and watched their boots,
Thick-dusted from the threshing field,
Their dusty trousers on the floor.

The Furnace

Sometimes my father pissed into the coals.
It made no difference: when shovelled from
The dark recess, the granules smoked a bit
Then glowed like hell-fire in the bellows' roar.
The long arm with the cow-horn handle creaked;
Somewhere behind, the leathers wheezed and groaned
And uttered blue-edged flames that stroked the crust
Of crumbling coal towards white heat. There at
The heart was iron, lost, till his hand fetched
It back on tongs and hammered it. Hardening,
It chimed, a new thing, won from rust.

The Well

'You'll never bring him up, my dear:
That vein across his little nose —
A sign he'll drown.'
                              The coverlet,
The pillow, and the small face blurred.
She held the handle hard, the pram
Her only anchor in a world
In flood. 'I'm sorry, dear, to tell
You this, but that's a sign.'
                              Then she
Was walking home, old Biah gone,
Her crow's garb gone, her white face gone,
Her words not gone, never to go.

You dropped a stone in, and the sound
Came up a long time afterwards,
A cold sound, dark, that frightened you
To make you look and drop again.
Lean over far enough, and far,
Far down, a face looked up at you.
You broke it with a stone.

The pail went lolloping down, banging
The dark green sides, until it tipped
And sank. You wound it up slowly,
Not to spill. There was another way.
Let go, the iron handle spun,
The chain raced off the roller and
The pail fell straight. After the jerk,
The chain was tight, down there the pail
Suspended still. Winding, you looked
For its coming back, the glimmering

About to break the surface, felt
Something like welcome for it when
It spilt its silver round the rim.

How long is 'bringing up'? she wondered
As the years passed, watched the vein,
Less noticeable as boyhood came.
Was there a time beyond which all
Harm's ways were barred? the pond outside
The door, the well, the summer sea,
And all the unknown places dared
In urchin hours? Tom scoffed, but built
A wooden structure on the well,
With bolted door. 'These bloody old
Wives' tales.' But some were sometimes true.

In time, the bolt stayed drawn, the door
Even lay open carelessly.
(Once, a rat was found, floating,
The water left untouched for days.)
The curious stones dropped in, and soon
The pail, wound on a chain of trust
In what was normal for a boy —
Who did not drown.

                Disused for years,
The well has been filled in, rubble
And soil have proved it shallower
Than a boy's imaginings.
He'll not drown here.
                The vein still shows,
The more when tension comes, though five
Decades have gone. He wonders sometimes if
Old Biah had the superstition wrong,
If some dark water waits him still.
The hand that held the pram will never know.

Ex-Army Bicycles, Norfolk, 1930's

1
The bicycle was high, the wheels
Turned smoothly when you spun them, on
And on; the leather saddle held
Your foot for perfect balancing,
One arm to guide, one outstretched, waved
In that applauding air.

2
Behind the barn, by nettle, dock,
In elder-shade, it leaned into
Its camouflage, a slung bag from
The side-turned handlebar.

3
In twos and threes, late afternoon,
Bent against wind or weariness,
They came on their Great War bicycles,
Eighteen and more years gone, some still
In army greatcoats, for no show
But warmth their wages would not buy,
The men who fought, and never heard
Of Owen, Rosenberg, Sassoon.

The Desk

The desk was high, Victorian, long disused;
One day, alone, some nine years old, he opened it.
The smell was oil, old iron, rope, and dirt, the wood
Paler inside, unaged. He turned things over, then
Stopped short, his fingers faltering upon a page
Of dark One Penny stamps, the young Queen's head
   profiled
Against the background sepia. He closed the lid,
Went through the winding shadows to the light outside.

Noah's Flood

'It rained for forty days and nights' . . . and so
Out there beyond the high window
It did, in our imaginations, grey-
Brown water rising till the village lay
Submerged in Noah's Flood. The ark was made
In our own yard; long planks of poplar laid
End-on made do for gopher wood; the beasts
Stayed safely vague and credible; south-east,
Near Diss, lay Ararat; on Ashton's roof
Of red, washed tiles, I saw the dove.

Lavengro

All day, the sun in the foundry yard:
On corrugated-iron roofs
Of shelters for the seasoning wood,
A threshing drum, the early Ford;
On elder, nettle, orchard; on
Lavengro. Pages turn, and my
Lank fifteen years sprawled in the grass
Follow those far-off dusty roads
To Mumpers' Dingle. It is night
Though the foundry roofs burn still.
My Romany tongue charms Isopel.

The Workshop Door

The long day's painting done,
Old threshing drums and strawpitchers made new,
They wiped their brushes on the workshop door.

The random glazes, scumbles, gleamed
Scarlet or yellow ochre, green, behind
The bushel skeps, sack barrow, and corn scales.

They brushed the years on, texturing
A patch like tiny cobblestones
That more than any picture then

Instructed me. Years afterwards,
Nineteen or so, I'd stand and contemplate
Hendrickje Stoffels in an amber glow

Near Norwich Market Place, an artshop print
That lured me to the window where she smiled,
Or almost smiled, from Rembrandt's shadows

On most Saturdays. What pulled was not
The secret flesh, subsumed in that warm gaze,
Not that alone, but pigment, brushstroke, glaze.

The Stairway

Find where it leads, this stairway, steps worn thin
Precarious, a ladder, not much more,
Pitched sharply up. Open the door.

The dust unsettles. Breathe two centuries
Held here by grey floorboard, grimed whitewashed wall,
Beneath bare roof-tiles. Your footfall

Is my family's. The grubby light
Picks out their artefacts, the rusted rings,
The nuts and bolts, dark iron things

That fastened England. Go down, and leave them here.
Remark again how worn the steps are, thin
With their ghostly trafficking.

The Hammer

My father's hands;
The hammer held, then ringing down
On tempered steel; the chisel-head
Burred over; grime on skin;
Two knuckles red,
Small customary wounds,
Not much to make a poem of —
Summoning a too-late love.

Other Poems

Arab Women with Child
— *Kokoschka*

'Don't look at her: look here, at me,'
She seems to say. 'I am the mystery
Of deserts — let me lure you, painting man,
Your squinting eye, your brush. Where can
You find my like in this dry place,
My vivid robe, my young uncovered face?'

The other holds her child. 'See how
He stands for you — paint him. The breasts I show
Are desert gourds. She soon will find
The good flesh gone, her skin a rind.
I had no like in this dry place,
My vivid robe, my young uncovered face.'

A Bakst Nude

Sleeping there
in Bakst's small water-colour,
nude, and utterly displayed,

you are changed somehow
from a merely naked girl
who happened to pose

by the date against his signature
at the cushion-edge,
touched lightly in

when he told you to open eyes
and end the make-believe:
1914.

Deux jeunes filles lisant

We turn the page. She reads the words
That will not pass my eyes, shape thoughts
I want to share, make images
I want to hold, as I hold her,
Would still, in these calm moments here,
After. Suppose the selfsame words
The selfsame moment registered:
To be so close . . . They'd go their own
Ways though, divide inside our heads
Like travellers on different roads.

Her places are not mine, Provence,
The little farms I've seen from trains,
Her faces, voices, houses, trees,
Her sea, her bare brown limbs — a child,
Her little schoolroom, books, her bed,
The birds beneath the eaves . . .

The traffic drones outside, a plane
High up, like God, goes South
Because it always goes at four . . .
She looks at me and smiles. I smile.
We turn the page.

In half an hour we'll dress. I'll be
Bonnard, I'll watch her go
From room to room, a barefoot nude,
In light and shadow by the door,
The yellows, mauves, her amber skin,
Reach up, unwind the towel, let
Her hair fall, go against the glass
And comb and comb, bend to the drawer

And take her clothes, and turn to me.
I'll stand where she stood, and she'll say
'You're beautiful. Get dressed.' She'll see
In her way only, artless, crude:
I'll never be more than I am
Through her eyes, never light and dark,
A turning line across a page,
Mysterious and real . . .

                    One day
She'll leave, let some thick farmer roll
On top each night, breed beautiful
Brown children . . . *Le petit paysan* . . .
Blue-eyed, identical. I'll cry
Awhile. She'll write: *Come down and stay.*
Perhaps I'll go. *He's in the fields.*
I still read in the afternoon.
Sometimes I think of how you stood
In sunlight by the door. I try
To see as you would, like Bonnard.
It's easier now. I could not look
Sometimes — you were so actual.
I'd have you so again. Come soon.

She turns the page. Her face is blurred.
'Dreamer, you've hardly read a word.'

A Driftwood Pendant

Sandpaper off
the roughness, rub
away the patina
that sand and sea
have left.

Remove the blemishes,
but carefully:
retain the basic form
that sand and sea
have given it.

Consider what the sea
would work on next;
search out soft surfaces;
erode them gently:
be the sea.

Accentuate
the forms that interest;
subtly impose
intelligence
the sea could not.

Smooth down the whole.
Follow the grain;
refine each surface
equally. Return
again, again.

Next, use a seal
to bring out colour
and preserve; when dry,
sandpaper lightly,
and repeat.

The final stages: bore
a careful hole,
soften a thong,
thread on, and knot.
Now find a girl.

La Première sortie
— *Renoir*

How we would have forgotten the show,
Seen only her, still almost a child,
Unfocussed all those faces, row
On row beyond her, smiled
At her animation, hoped she might
For a moment turn her enchanted eyes
To follow us into the night
At curtain-fall and the lights' surprise.

The Bowl of Milk
— *Bonnard*

In a moment the little black cat will be gone,
The bowl of milk set down somewhere
Outside the picture-space. Alone
Upstairs, Marthe will undress, prepare
The ritual water, soap herself, and lie,
Becoming innocent. The cat will drop
Asleep in the sun, the milk bowl dry.
Bonnard will paint sunlight on the table top.

The Ice Hill

'There is a green hill far away',
We sang in school. It stood
Not far, but where four meadows met
On Bush's farm, a mound
We called the Ice Hill. Legend said
Our ancestors kept meat
On hoarded ice there. Sceptical,
We still kept it from thaw.

Bush doubted too. The farm was poor:
It was not avarice
That lured, but commonsense; and sense
Of history. A place
Of burial, some said, and Bush
Dreamed bracelet, torque, and pence
About piled bones. We found his shaft,
Through clay, steep centuries down.

And nothing there. The copse around
Was alien. We went,
Feared Bush, pervading his dark hill.
'Forgive . . . our trespasses,
As we . . .' Yet something sent
Us trespassing, until
The digging had long stopped. That year
The hole seemed shallower.

Children's Questions

1 *Julian, 4*

We follow down the turning stair
Into a room far underground,
Regard the scratched stone walls, sense fear
And horror grained on every inch.
'If you will keep your children near,
I'll put the light out, so you'll see
How dark it was.' A switch somewhere
Imprisons us. The dungeon's dark
Is absolute. Silenced, we hear
The nothing prisoners heard, watch for
The glimmering that should appear
When eyes have grown accustomed. Close,
A child whispers, 'Are we still here?'

2 *Marina, 10*

'How do we know,' the child asked, 'that
We're not dreaming all this?' — meaning
The world, our whole experience.
Ten years of living shaped the thought;
Ten more have hidden what I said.
Perhaps it was, 'The world seems real.'
'Perhaps our dreams are real,' she said.

Old Man in a Pine Tree

An old man is sawing a tree,
the tall ladder almost vertical
against the branch he lops
of its sere extremity.

Unsatisfied, he mounts
to four rungs from the top,
straddles the bough,
a boy again,

and reaches up and out
and saws still higher now,
then, back upon the rung,
faces about,

lops all he reaches, lost
in his intent from age
and fear, the ladder steadier
than when he mounted it.

Up one more rung, and then
another, holding on
and leaning far, he saws
beyond all cautioning.

I write this as he works,
and finish as he throws
the saw lightly to ground
and turns, and looks

on roofs among
the gardens round
he must descend to,
slowly, slowly, ageing rung by rung.

A Later Season

A poor stick nest,
Revealed when leaves are gone,
Perches precariously.
The bough is thin,
A horizontal balancing
The shoddy, pitched thing.

Cranking home,
I think of what's undone,
Ideas abandoned, shown
Up suddenly in light
Of a later season.

Old Ground

These are the first graves for
Two centuries, on this south side.
The church has stood six more.

The seasons are long,
But planting time's come round.

Winter Reeds

Few things seem more worth
A scatter of recalcitrant words
Than this dry clump of reeds —

Not as that heaped couch-grass
Hardy recalled, in age:
'Yet this will go onward the same' —

No, not that thought, but how,
A month ago, they stood
In deep, fresh-fallen snow,
A Chinese brushwork, on
A perfect page.

Heard in a Sussex Drawing Room

That you admire my verse
Gives me no pleasure:
Prolix or terse,
I have my own measure.

My books are not diminished
That they stay on the shelf:
When a poem's finished,
I don't read it myself.

This 'truth' you think I write —
It's mostly fiction:
Facts wouldn't carry quite
The same conviction.

After Drouth

Lately, he wrote again,
Struggling from long drouth,
Not lines of sour old age —
He'd written them in youth —
Not runes to outface death,
Not lust's declining rage —
No, not a word of these:
Small songs, he wrote, the breath
A child makes on cold glass
Before bedtime, turned plain
And marvellous by frost.

The Imaginative Franchise

'. . . the peculiar truth of poetry may have to be rendered by fictions, or by what, literally, amounts to lies . . .'
Michael Hamburger, *The Truth of Poetry*

Does it matter, whether Yeats really stood
Among schoolchildren? Lawrence's snake
Could as easily have slithered out of his skull
As out of that fissure. Were there woods
Frost stopped his horse by, and did there fall
The 'darkest evening'? Had Larkin a bike?
Does it have to be true? Suppose the train did not pull
Up at Adlestrop at all . . .